FAVORITE SONGS

Sing in the Barbershop Quartet — Volume 3

CONTENTS

Beginning pitches on the CD are the root (tonic) of the song's key.

ISBN 978-1-4234-6181-4

HAL•LEONARD®
CORPORATION

7777 W. BLUEMOUND RD. P.O. BOX 13819 MILWAUKEE, WI 53213

Visit Hal Leonard Online at
www.halleonard.com

Coney Island Baby/We All Fall

Arranged by
SPEBSQSA, Inc.

CONEY ISLAND BABY
Words and Music by LES APPLETON

WE ALL FALL
Words and Music by GEORGE GOODWIN
and GEORGE W. MEYER

some girl that dress - es neat,   some girl that's got big feet,

19   girl   some girl   we

we meet her on the street. Then we'll join the

21   meet   ar -

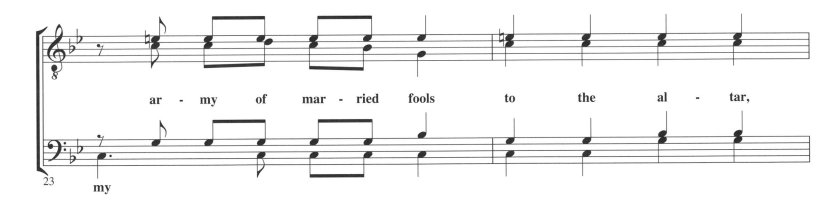

ar - my of mar - ried fools to the al - tar,

23   my

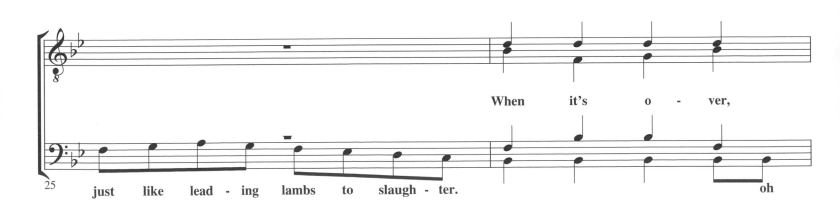

When it's o - ver,

25   just like lead - ing lambs to slaugh - ter.   oh

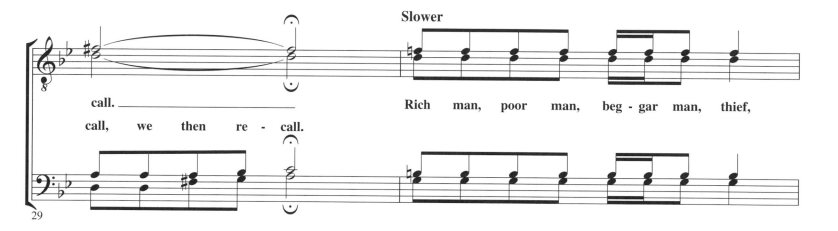

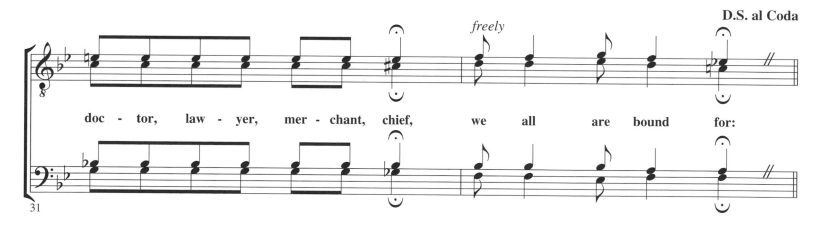

He's Got the Whole World in His Hands

**Arrangement by
FRED KING**

Traditional Spiritual

He's got the whole world __ in His hands, He's got the whole wide world __

in His hands, He's got the whole world __ in His hands, __ whole world in His

hands.

Bm ba bm bm, He's got the wind and the rain in His hands, __ wind and the rain

in His hands, He's got the wind and the rain in His hands, __ whole world in His hands. __

Hey, Little Baby o' Mine

Arrangement by
JOE LILES

Words and Music by
JOE LILES

12

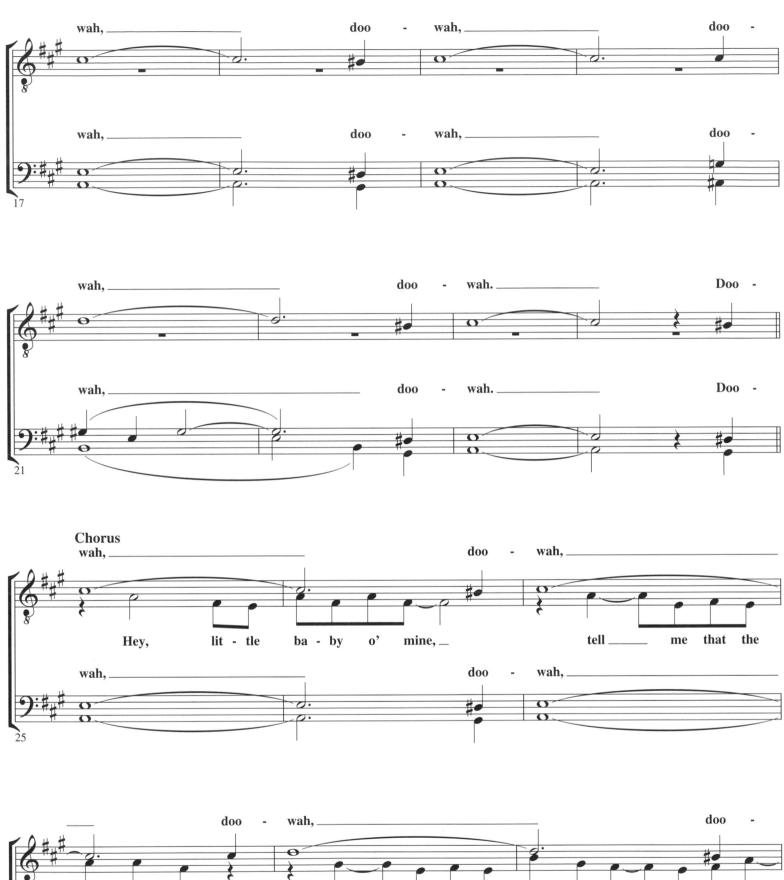

13

14

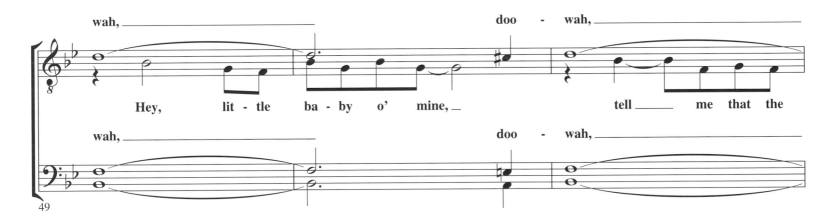

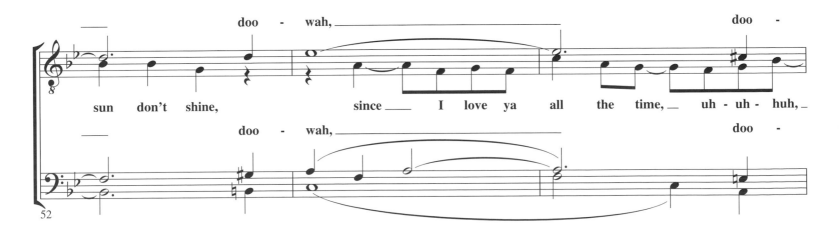

In the Good Old Summertime

Arrangement by
SPEBSQSA, Inc.

Words by REN SHIELDS
Music by GEORGE EVANS

beau - ti - ful   rhyme.

rhyme. _____   No   trou - ble   an - noy - ing,   each   one   is   en -

beau - ti - ful   rhyme.

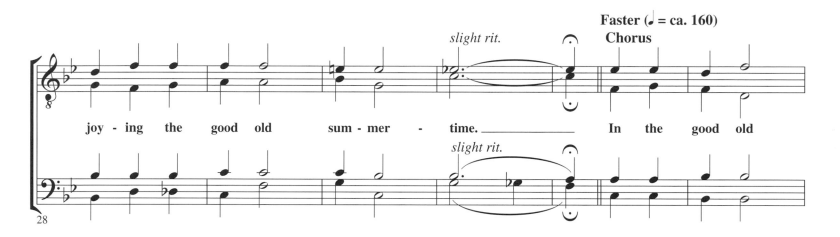

slight rit.   **Faster (♩ = ca. 160)**
Chorus

joy - ing   the   good old   sum - mer - time. _____   In   the   good   old

slight rit.

sum - mer -

sum - mer - time, _____   in   the   good   old   sum - mer - time, _____

sum - mer -

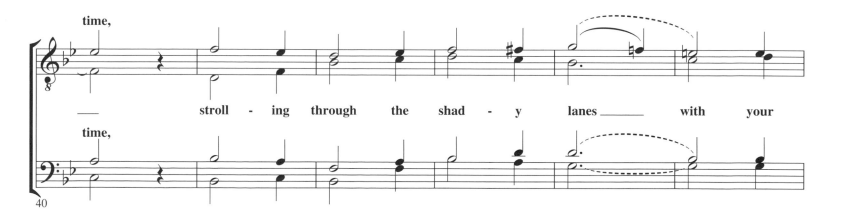

time,

___   stroll - ing   through   the   shad - y   lanes ___   with   your

time,

20

ba - by mine._____ You hold her hand and she holds

yours and that's a ver - y good sign_____ that she's your

toot - sey woot - sey in the good old sum - mer - time.

Tag
Slower *tenor melody*

In the good old sum - mer - time._____

Water Is Wide

Arrangement by
RICK SPENCER

Traditional

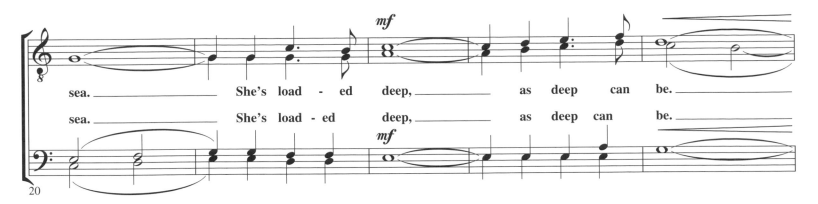

sea. _____ She's load - ed deep, _____ as deep can be.

sea. _____ She's load - ed deep, _____ as deep can be. _____

_____ But not as deep _____ as the love I'm in, _____ I know not

_____ But not as deep _____ as the love I'm in, _____ I know not

deep as deep as the love I'm in, _____ I know not

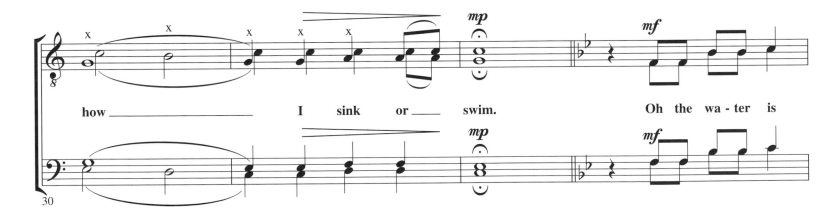

how _____ I sink or _____ swim. Oh the wa - ter is

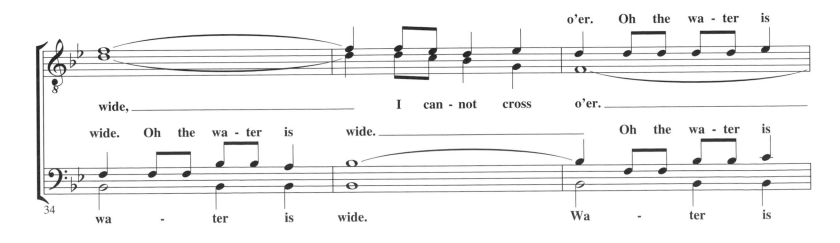

o'er. Oh the wa - ter is

wide, _____ I can - not cross o'er. _____

wide. Oh the wa - ter is wide. _____ Oh the wa - ter is

wa - ter is wide. Wa - ter is

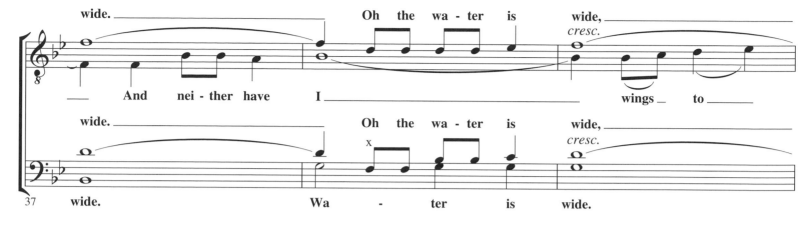

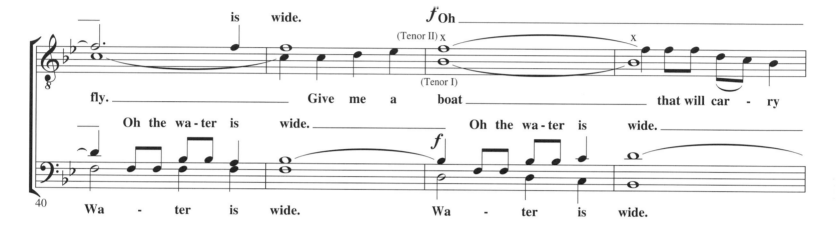

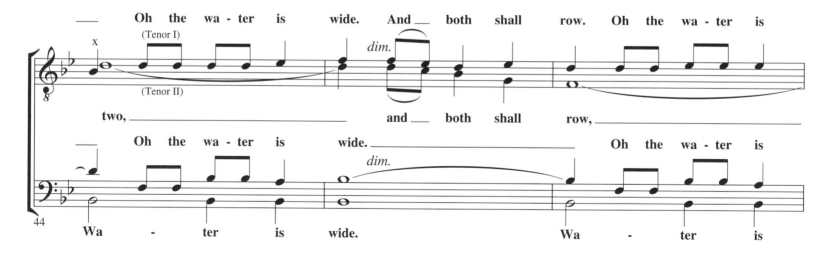

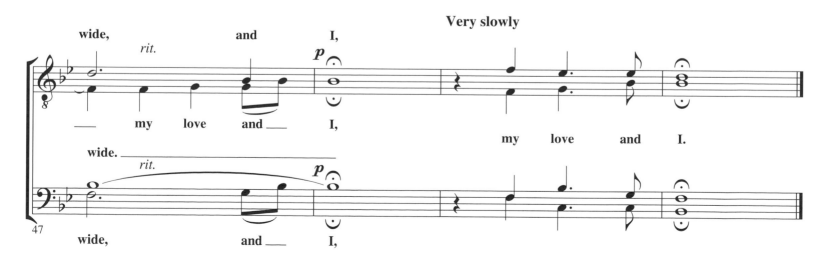

The Star Spangled Banner

Arrangement by
VAL J. HICKS

Words by FRANCIS SCOTT KEY
Music by JOHN STAFFORD SMITH

Take Me Out to the Ball Game

Arrangement by
SPEBSQSA, Inc.

Words by JACK NORWORTH
Music by ALBERT von TILZER

This Little Light of Mine/Do Lord

**Arrangment by
VAL J. HICKS**

Traditional

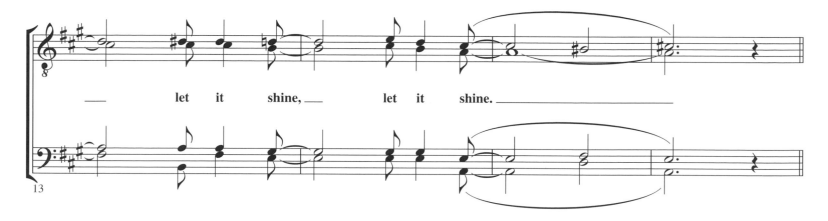

let it shine, ___ let it shine. _____

DO LORD
Slightly faster (♩ = ca. 130)

mf I've got a home in Glo-ry Land__ that out-shines the sun.

mf (Oh, broth-er,)

I've got a home in Glo-ry Land__ that out-shines the sun.

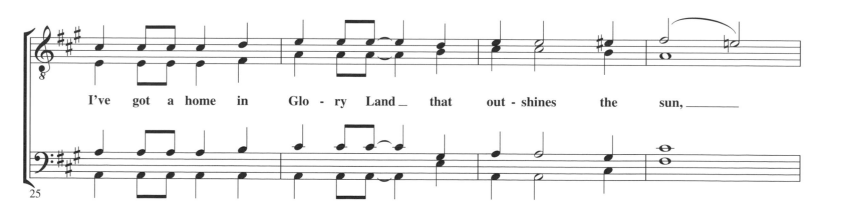

I've got a home in Glo-ry Land__ that out-shines the sun, _____

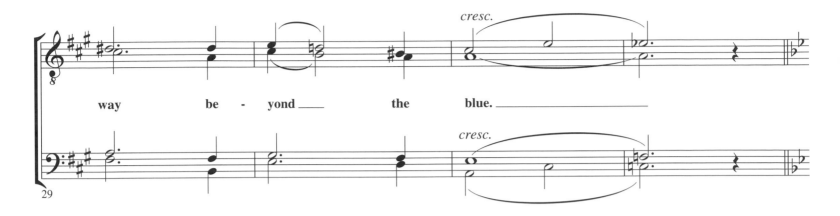

way be - yond _____ the blue. _____

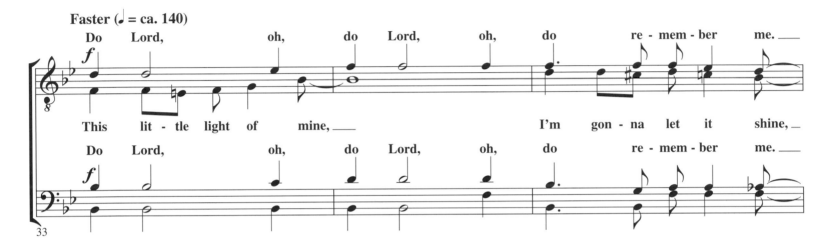

Faster (♩ = ca. 140)

Do Lord, oh, do Lord, oh, do re - mem - ber me. _____

This lit - tle light of mine, _____ I'm gon - na let it shine, _____

Do Lord, oh, do Lord, oh, do re - mem - ber me. _____

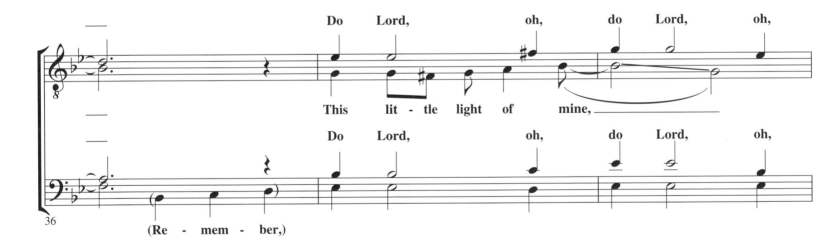

Do Lord, oh, do Lord, oh,

This lit - tle light of mine, _____

Do Lord, oh, do Lord, oh,

(Re - mem - ber,)

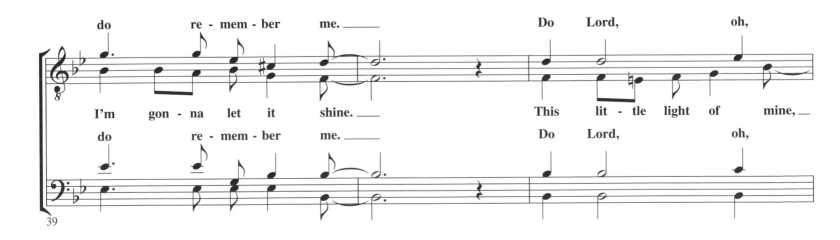

do re - mem - ber me. _____ Do Lord, oh,

I'm gon - na let it shine. _____ This lit - tle light of mine, _____

do re - mem - ber me. _____ Do Lord, oh,

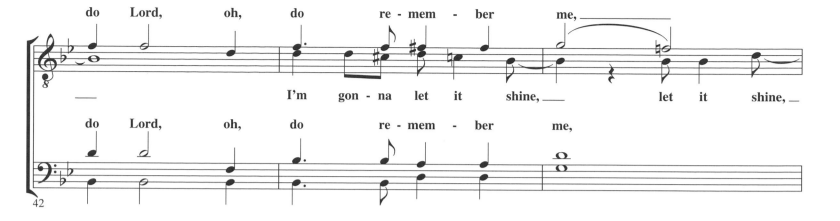

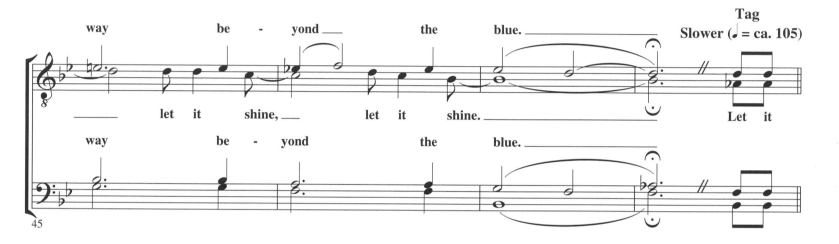

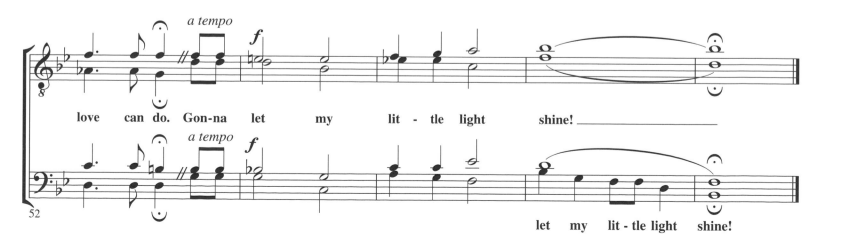

SING WITH THE CHOIR

CD INCLUDED

These **GREAT COLLECTIONS** let singers
BECOME PART OF A FULL CHOIR and sing along
with some of the most-loved songs of all time.
Each book includes SATB parts (arrangements are enlarged from octavo-size to 9" x 12")
and the accompanying CD features full, professionally recorded performances.

Now you just need to turn on the CD, open the book, pick your part, and
SING ALONG WITH THE CHOIR!

1. ANDREW LLOYD WEBBER
Any Dream Will Do • As If We Never Said Good-bye • Don't Cry for Me Argentina • Love Changes Everything • Memory • The Music of the Night • Pie Jesu • Whistle down the Wind.
00333001 Book/CD Pack.............................. $14.95

2. BROADWAY
Bring Him Home • Cabaret • For Good • Luck Be a Lady • Seasons of Love • There's No Business like Show Business • Where Is Love? • You'll Never Walk Alone.
00333002 Book/CD Pack.............................. $14.95

3. STANDARDS
Cheek to Cheek • Georgia on My Mind • I Left My Heart in San Francisco • I'm Beginning to See the Light • Moon River • On the Sunny Side of the Street • Skylark • When I Fall in Love.
00333003 Book/CD Pack.............................. $14.95

4. THE 1950S
At the Hop • The Great Pretender • Kansas City • La Bamba • Love Me Tender • My Prayer • Rock Around the Clock • Unchained Melody.
00333004 Book/CD Pack.............................. $14.95

5. THE 1960S
All You Need is Love • Can't Help Falling in Love • Dancing in the Street • Good Vibrations • I Heard It Through the Grapevine • I'm a Believer • Under the Boardwalk • What a Wonderful World.
00333005 Book/CD Pack.............................. $14.95

6. THE 1970S
Ain't No Mountain High Enough • Bohemian Rhapsody • I'll Be There • Imagine • Let It Be • Night Fever • Yesterday Once More • You Are the Sunshine of My Life.
00333006 Book/CD Pack.............................. $14.95

7. DISNEY FAVORITES
The Bare Necessities • Be Our Guest • Circle of Life • Cruella De Vil • Friend like Me • Hakuna Matata • Joyful, Joyful • Under the Sea.
00333007 Book/CD Pack.............................. $14.95

8. DISNEY HITS
Beauty and the Beast • Breaking Free • Can You Feel the Love Tonight • Candle on the Water • Colors of the Wind • A Whole New World (Aladdin's Theme) • You'll Be in My Heart • You've Got a Friend in Me.
00333008 Book/CD Pack.............................. $14.95

9. LES MISÉRABLES
At the End of the Day • Bring Him Home • Castle on a Cloud • Do You Hear the People Sing? • Finale • I Dreamed a Dream • On My Own • One Day More.
00333009 Book/CD Pack.............................. $14.95

10. CHRISTMAS FAVORITES
Frosty the Snow Man • The Holiday Season • (There's No Place Like) Home for the Holidays • Little Saint Nick • Merry Christmas, Darling • Santa Claus Is Comin' to Town • Silver Bells • White Christmas.
00333011 Book/CD Pack.............................. $14.95

11. CHRISTMAS TIME IS HERE
Blue Christmas • Christmas Time is Here • Feliz Navidad • Happy Xmas (War Is Over) • I'll Be Home for Christmas • Let It Snow! Let It Snow! Let It Snow! • We Need a Little Christmas • Wonderful Christmastime.
00333012 Book/CD Pack.............................. $14.95

FOR MORE INFORMATION, SEE YOUR LOCAL MUSIC DEALER, OR WRITE TO:

HAL • LEONARD® CORPORATION
7777 W. BLUEMOUND RD. P.O. BOX 13819 MILWAUKEE, WI 53213

Prices, contents, and availability
subject to change without notice.

0508